IN THE BEGINNING
THE EPIC OF THE ANUNNAKI

Alex Teplish
Writer and Creator

Edwin Chavez
+
Shipeng Lee Studio
Illustrators

Oana V.
of
DeveoMedia Studio
Colorist

Zach Berger
+
Marcelo A. Orsi Blanco
Cover Artists

Cover, introduction, artwork and compilation Copyright © 2013 Alex Teplish. All Rights Reserved.
The stories, characters, and incidents featured in this publication are entirely fictional.

Printed in China

This book is dedicated to my wife, Melaina, my daughters, Sasha and Mia, and the rest of my family and friends. You have all shown me support, interest, and love throughout my creative process, which helped me pursue and complete this project.

INTRODUCTION

For as long as writing has existed, humans have recorded their experiences and history for future generations. At first, pictographs were used to depict people's surroundings and what they saw. Early civilizations eventually converted these pictures into symbols representing sounds, rather than exact things or objects. Prior to mo[dern] human technological or scientific discoveries, humans could not descri[be] everything they experienced using their existing symbols or words. Instead, they used their limited vocabulary to discuss what was not yet understood. As time passed, a multitude of written accounts survived to be translated in our day. Unfortunately, a lot more were destroyed or decayed over the vast time span of history.

Many of the more ancient and outrageous stories are now dismissed as myths and legends, while the more accepted miraculous stories have been taken on by a variety of religions. Some theorists delve deeper into these stories and propose an alternative history, on[e] with an ancient extraterrestrial influence. There are others yet, wh[o] speculate that there exists a hidden code in the Bible. Like looking int[o] a crystal, these mysterious texts may indeed have many facets, bein[g] a story within a story within a story. Regardless of which theory on[e] subscribes to, evidence shows that some major events took place thousands of years ago that influenced cultures around the world.

One of the ancient astronaut theories suggests that many years ago a group of humanoid beings from another planet came to Earth in search of their desired resources. They are known as the Anunnaki an[d] had extremely long life spans. Using their advanced genetic technique[s] they created various worker beings to take on the harsh conditions o[f] intense labor needed on Earth. These new beings were a mix of the existing hominids that evolved on Earth and their own Anunnaki DNA[.] Like an upgrade to software, our earlier ancestors took an evolutionar[y] jump into what they would have evolved to over many years. As time went by, the worker beings were improved upo[n] and utilized for a variety of purposes to serve their creators. These new humans became almost biologically [like the] indistinguishable from the Anunnaki, with the differences being superficial, but they also lacked longevity and scientific knowledg[e]

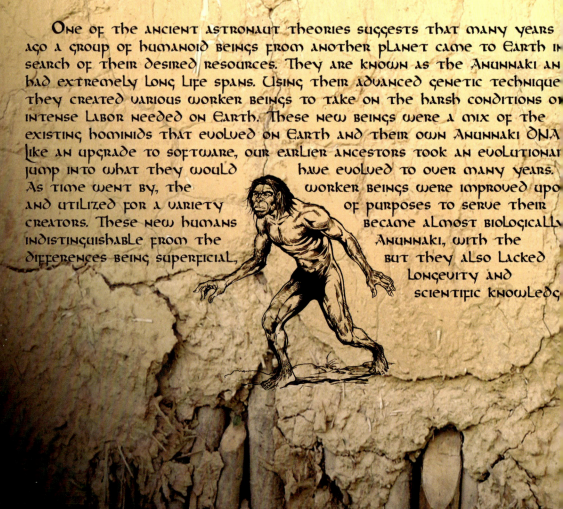

As thousands of years progressed, many humans lived a simple life　due to the advanced technology of the Anunnaki, revered and　nsidered them as gods or angels. The first civilization known to have　corded history and their daily lives, the Sumerians, attributed much　 their sudden knowledge as having been taught to them by the　ods". There are parallels in most ancient, supposedly, unrelated　ltures and religions that describe these "gods" and their time spent　 Earth. Many theorists speculate that the misinterpretations of the　st along with a spiritual yearning, led to the various religions,　yths, and legends we know of today.

The word, god, itself has come to mean many things. To some of　e older religions, there were many gods, while the monotheistic　ligions that followed, considered there to be one encompassing　eator of all. An omnipotent god can still exist alongside the ancient　tronaut theory. All creation, including extraterrestrials and their　tions, would all stem from such an omnipotent god. The moral　ects of these belief structures can still be applied, it's the stories　emselves that may have been misunderstood over time. Based on　antum physics, every particle is connected to one another and is　de of energy. This energy in its entirety, or the creation force　elf, can potentially have a supreme consciousness. Just as an ant　nnot fathom a human's experience, we may not be able to fathom　at lies beyond our own evolutionary scale, especially at its utmost　treme.

In recent history, there has been a phenomenon called "cargo　ts". These are new religions, cults, or myths formed by indigenous　bes that were not familiar with the modern world. They would　 planes fly by, soldiers landing on their islands, or cargo being　dropped, sometimes interacting with soldiers　emselves. These people interpreted such things as　stical and formed new religions/cults based on　at they saw. They even built replica　planes, rifles, and landing strips out of their　al raw materials in hopes that the soldiers　uld return and provide them with more　ful goods. Similarly, the　ients may have seen technology　ey could not understand and　interpreted it, adding it into their　ical and mythological stories.

This book is not meant to have any negative intentions toward any race, culture, or religious group. We are all human beings living on Earth, trying to survive and be happy with the resources we have. Our history has molded us all, the mistakes of our past, and we continue to evolve our newly formed global society. I do not believe that any one race or religion is completely right or superior over another. Humanity's general surroundings and circumstances have led people to do both good and bad things. Those who have done good or created something positive for society come from all over the world with diverse backgrounds and religions. Many treat their scriptures as allegories, interpreting them into morals and applying them to their lives. Such people use their beliefs as lessons to help others, which is beneficial to society. Those who use their biblical stories to discriminate, or worse yet, act out in violence are the ones that have held back mankind's development. People from anti-religious backgrounds have also done horrible things in the course of history over their belief in superiority. Sometimes, our beliefs create invisible borders that give us the illusion of separation.

How can so many people around the world be convinced that their interpretations of reality or spirituality be the true one while all others are incorrect? Even within the major religions, there are sects that disagree with each other's interpretations. Is it not the circumstances we are each born into, that determine what belief system we are taught? Do most actually get an opportunity to explore a diverse set of beliefs from early childhood? Majority of the world has been stuck in the same cycle, where they have been taught as children not to doubt their teachings, while accepting certain dogmas to be true. Can a person truly have free will if they are taught from birth that their culture is right while others are wrong or possibly evil? I have therefore come to understand that a belief is more like a strong opinion on topics we haven't truly proven. We should all be entitled to one, but not impose it with force on others. True freedom is when we can explore one another's beliefs and come up with our own conclusions. Just like the rest of nature, our belief system should evolve over time, as one trait overcomes another combining spirituality with science. I therefore encourage all readers to do your own research and think for yourselves.

The story in this book is a work of fiction, but is based on actual theories by those from a variety of educated backgrounds that consider the basis to be a possibility. Do I truly believe in this? For me to believe something to be accurate and true I must be a witness to the fact, be informed by someone I trust, or see no reason for it not to be. Even with those we trust, there are times people have been known to misinterpret, be fooled, or mistaken. I, therefore, consider there to be many possibilities to what happened in our ancient past. This particular theory, one of the ancient astronaut influence on Earth, is one of those possibilities that I think to be plausible. While believing this to be a possibility, I can honestly say that it's also possible that it is not true or perfectly accurate. Rather than settle on one group of people's outlook, even my own, I prefer to continue exploring and learning. Even with the scientific method along with many studies, later discoveries sometimes prove their predecessors to be incorrect. That doesn't mean we should discount science, as it is the best method for a practical understanding of the universe we are a part of.

The general concepts of this story are primarily based on Zecharia Sitchin's theories, other related books and translations, in addition to stories from the book of Genesis. Using these subjects, I have added my own ideas as far as the situations, character traits, and conversations are concerned. I highly recommend reading the non-fiction works written about this theory, to learn more about this fascinating subject. "The Beginning" is the epic of the Anunnaki, depicting Enki and other Gods, described by the ancient Sumerians, and illustrates how their ancient astronaut journey all began.

Enjoy and keep exploring!

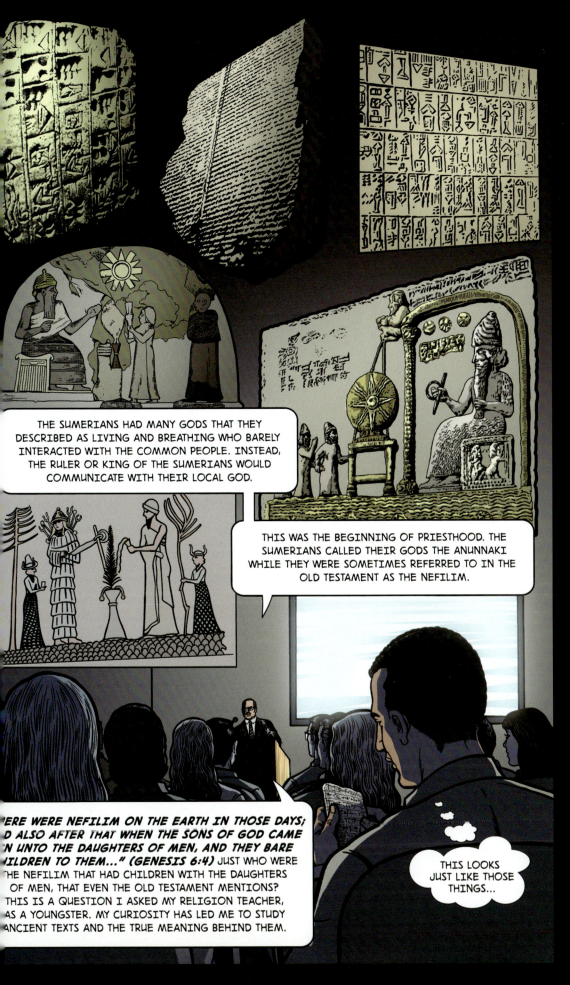

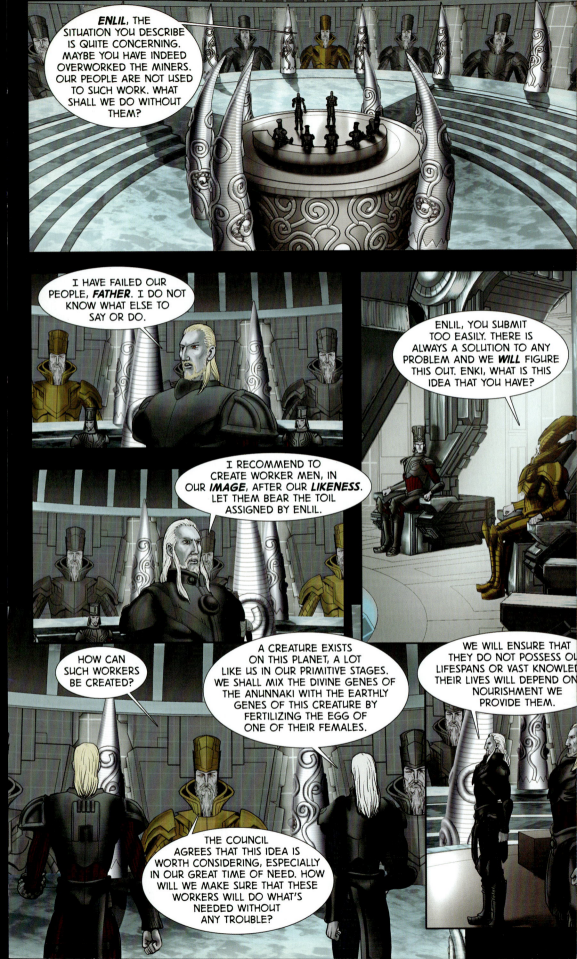

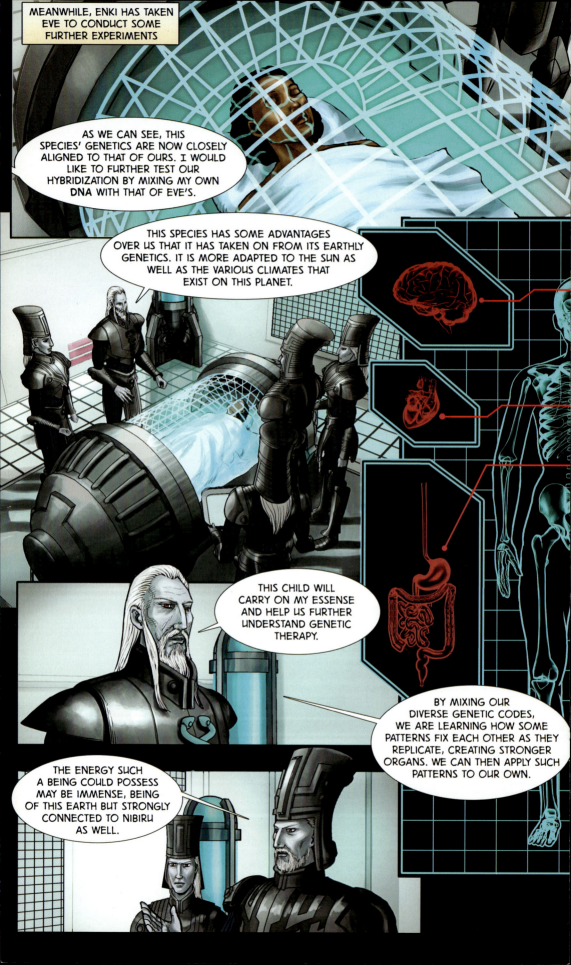

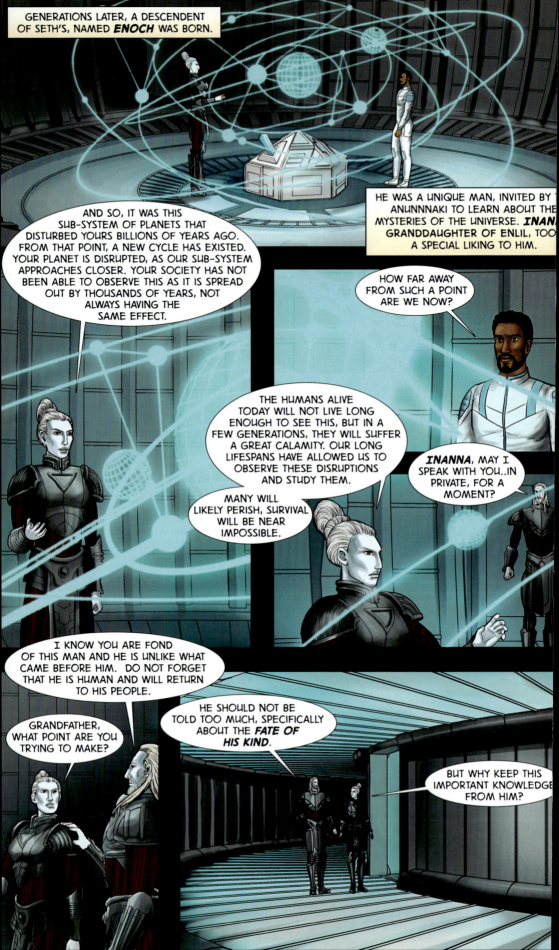

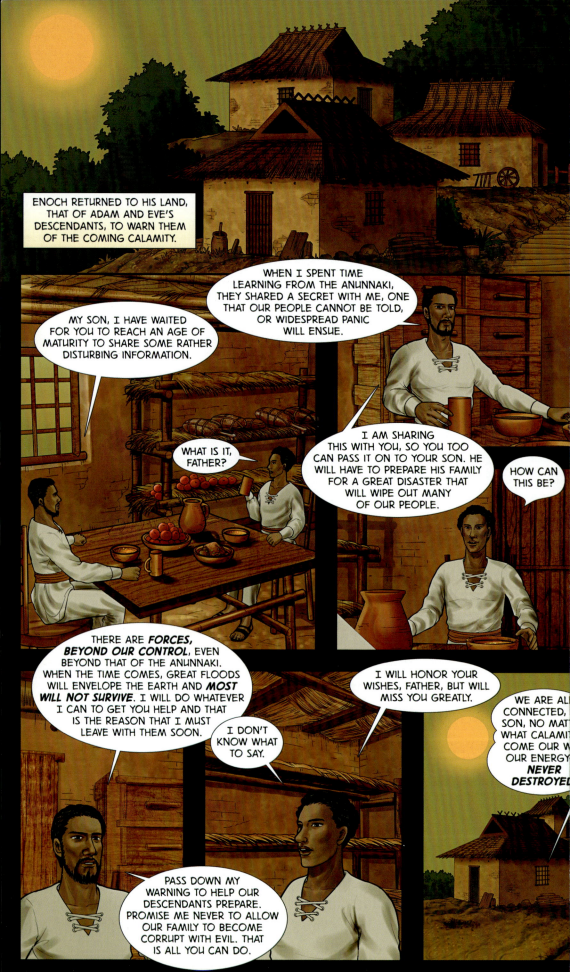

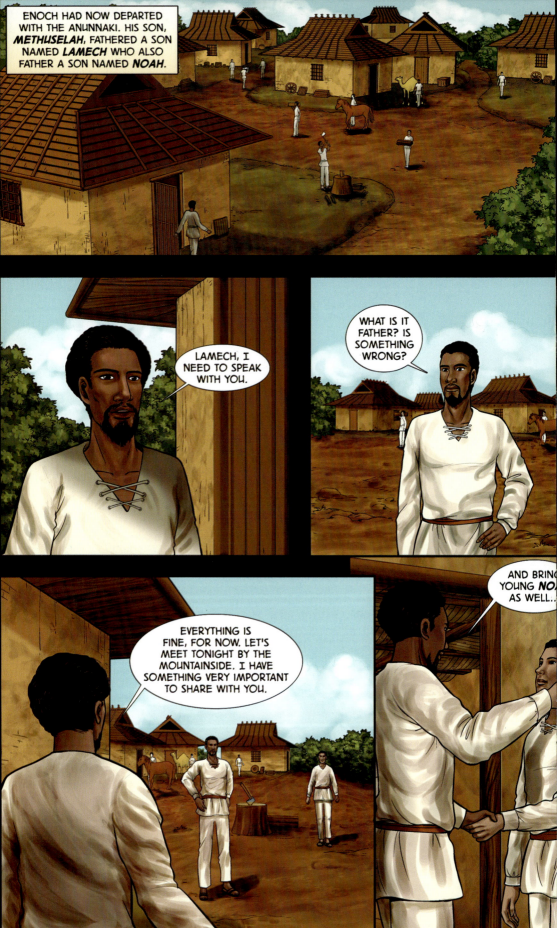

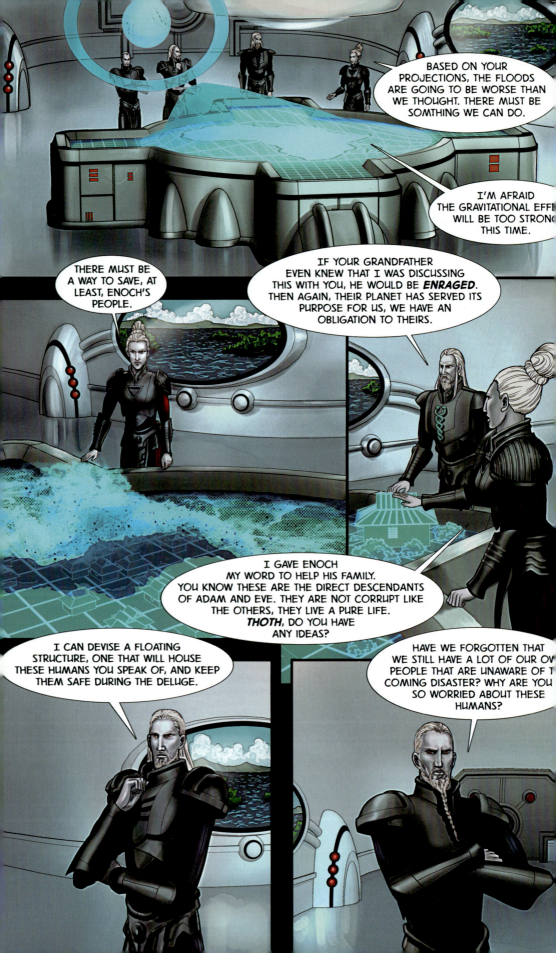

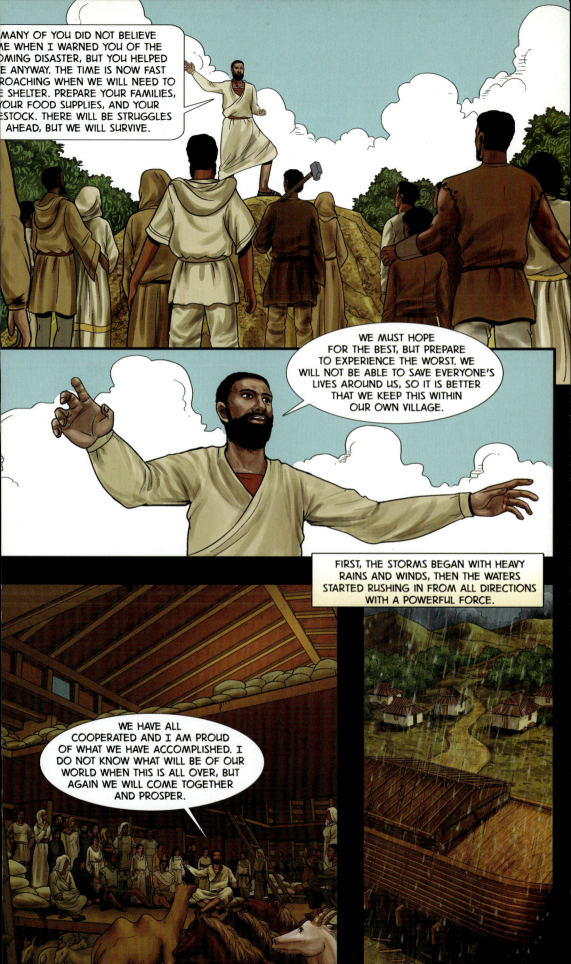

Suggested Books

The Earth Chronicles
Book I: Twelfth Planet
Book III: The Wars of Gods and Men
Book V: When Time Began
Book VI: Cosmic Code
Genesis Revisited
Divine Encounters
Zecharia Sitchin

Chariots of the Gods
Erich von Däniken

The Gods of Eden
William Bramley

Gods of the New Millennium
Alan F. Alford

Behold a Pale Horse
William Cooper

Alien Agenda
Jim Marrs

IN THE BEGINNING
THE EPIC OF THE ANUNNAKI

FOR MORE CONTENT GO TO
WWW.INTHEBEGINNINGTHEBOOK.COM